HOW-TO
LIBRARY

CREATING HALLOWEEN CRAFTS

By Dana Meachen Rau • Illustrated by Kathleen Petelinsek

CHERRY LAKE PUBLISHING • ANN ARBOR, MICHIGAN

CHERRY LAKE
Publishing

Published in the United States of America by Cherry Lake Publishing
Ann Arbor, Michigan
www.cherrylakepublishing.com

Content Adviser: Dr. Julia Hovanec, Department of Arts Education and Crafts, Kutztown University of Pennsylvania, Kutztown, Pennsylvania

Photo Credits: Page 4, ©Andriy Petrenko/Dreamstime.com; page 5, ©George W. Bailey/Shutterstock, Inc.; page 6, ©Monkey Business Images/Shutterstock, Inc.; page 7, ©Kobby Dagan/Dreamstime.com; page 8, ©iStockphoto.com/kirin_photo; page 9, ©Edward Fielding/Dreamstime.com; page 29, ©Suprijono Suharjoto/Dreamstime.com.

Library of Congress Cataloging-in-Publication Data
Rau, Dana Meachen, 1971–
   Creating Halloween crafts / by Dana Meachen Rau.
      pages cm — (How-to library. Crafts)
   Includes bibliographical references and index.
   ISBN 978-1-62431-149-9 (lib. bdg.) —
ISBN 978-1-62431-281-6 (pbk.) — ISBN 978-1-62431-215-1 (e-book)
 1. Halloween decorations—Juvenile literature. 2. Handicraft—Juvenile literature. I. Title.
   TT900.H32R365 2014
   745.594'1646—dc23   2013011221

Cherry Lake Publishing would like to acknowledge the work of The Partnership for 21st Century Skills. Please visit www.p21.org for more information.

Printed in the United States of America
Corporate Graphics Inc.
July 2013
CLFA13

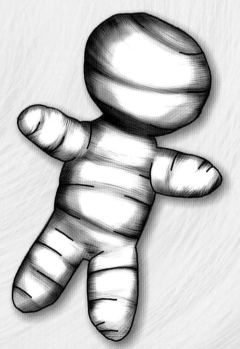

TABLE OF CONTENTS

Scary and Fun

Halloween arrives at the end of October every year. This holiday brings thrills, chills, candy, and fun. It is a time to dress up in costumes and imagine you are anything you want to be. You can be a superhero or a villain. You can be any sort of animal, from an elephant to a ladybug. You can be a pirate, a vampire, a princess, or even a cupcake. You can use your creativity to transform yourself for the night.

Halloween is a time for dressing in scary or silly costumes.

Some people hang decorations of ghosts, witches, and skeletons on doors and windows. Some people visit haunted houses. Many families wait until dark to ring doorbells and collect treats. Others go to parties where there are costume contests. They play games such as bobbing for apples, or carve pumpkins into jack-o'-lanterns. They play tricks and try not to eat too many treats!

A spooky jack-o'-lantern makes a great addition to your Halloween decorations.

Whether your celebrations are scary or fun (or both), you can use your creativity to make Halloween a memorable holiday.

An Ancient Holiday

Trick-or-treating is one of Halloween's most fun traditions.

Do you go trick-or-treating? Do you dress up in costumes? Many of our Halloween **traditions** have a long history. More than 2,000 years ago, the Celts of Europe celebrated a holiday a lot like our modern-day Halloween. They held a festival called Samhain (pronounced SAH-wun) that they celebrated around November 1. Samhain marked the end of the summer **harvest** and the beginning of winter.

The Celts believed that spirits of the dead came back to walk the earth during Samhain. People gathered around bonfires, wore costumes, danced, and paraded. They left gifts of food for the spirits. In the seventh century, the Christian church made Samhain a holiday to remember all the Christian saints. It was considered a holy, or "hallow," day. They called it All Hallows Day (later renamed All Saints' Day). The night before was All Hallows Eve, or Halloween. Today, we celebrate Halloween on October 31. November 1 is still All Saints' Day on the church calendar.

This Halloween, you might continue some of the ancient Celtic traditions. Trick-or-treaters dress up in costumes and go from house to house asking for candy. Figures of the dead, such as ghosts and skeletons, are still popular symbols of the holiday.

Many people use ghosts and other spooky symbols to decorate their houses for Halloween.

Halloween Inspiration

Creative people look for **inspiration**! Ideas for Halloween crafts and costumes are all around you. Costumes can be based on characters from movies, books, or shows. You can dress as people who have different jobs, such as astronauts, firefighters, or circus performers. You can dress as objects around the house, such as crayons, washing machines, or salt and pepper shakers. You can even dress as foods from your refrigerator!

You can be whatever you want on Halloween!

Some of the most popular costumes are also symbols of Halloween. These symbols make good decorations and Halloween displays. Transform yourself and your home with some of these symbols of the holiday:

- Bats
- Spiders
- Ravens, crows, owls, and vultures
- Black cats
- Frankenstein's monster and vampires
- Skeletons, ghosts, and mummies
- Wolves and werewolves
- Witches, pointed hats, cauldrons, and broomsticks
- Scarecrows, hay bales, and cornstalks
- Haunted houses, graveyards, tombstones, and full moons
- Pumpkins, gourds, apples, and nuts
- Dead leaves and cobwebs
- Candy corn, lollipops, chocolate bars, or any kind of candy!

HALLOWEEN COLORS
People often decorate for Halloween using the colors black, orange, purple, and green.

Candy corn is a delicious Halloween treat.

Basic Tools

Besides your inspiration and ideas, you will also need supplies to complete these projects!

Scissors, Box Cutter, Craft Knife

Scissors come in handy for many projects. A box cutter cuts through thick cardboard, and a craft knife is good for cutting small shapes out of paper. Always ask an adult for help when you need to use a box cutter or craft knife. These tools are very sharp. If you use a craft knife, you will also need a cutting mat so you don't cut your work surface.

Glue and Tape

Use white glue or glue sticks to attach paper to paper. A glue gun creates a stronger hold for heavier materials. It can get hot, so ask for an adult's help. Tape comes in a few types. Invisible tape is clear. Packing tape is wide, clear, and **durable**. Masking tape is tan and feels like paper. Duct tape is a thick, plastic fabric tape that is extra sticky and **flexible**.

Paper, Cardboard, Felt, Aluminum Foil

These materials can be cut, glued, and shaped to make a variety of costumes and crafts. For one of these projects you will need vellum paper. Vellum is a **translucent** paper that lets some light through. Aluminum foil is a shiny, thin sheet of metal.

Markers and Paint

Markers are good for adding details to your projects. Paint is better for larger areas. Water-based acrylic paint or poster paint makes cleanup easier. Fabric paints make permanent designs on fabric. If you are painting on your skin, use only paints specifically made for face painting.

Details

You can use many different items for costume and craft details. Bottle caps, beads, cotton balls, fabric scraps, yarn, string, streamers, balloons, and holiday lights can all be attached to your creations. Chenille sticks (also known as pipe cleaners) are a good addition to many projects. Craft sticks are short, flat, wooden sticks. Attach these details using glue, tape, or simple sewing stitches.

Make Your Own Costume

In October, stores are filled with premade Halloween costumes you can buy. But with just a few materials and a little creative thinking, you can make a costume yourself.

Large Cardboard Box

Use a box cutter (ask for an adult's help) to cut the flaps off the bottom of the box. Cut a hole for your head on the top and holes for your arms on each side. Decorate the box with paint and other details. Here are some ideas to help you get started:

- *Dice*: Paint the box white, and then draw black circles or glue on felt circles.
- *Robot*: Paint the box silver. Draw, paint, or glue on lids from jars and bottles to make buttons.
- *Television*: Do not cut a head hole. Instead, cut a rectangular hole in the front. Paint the box black, and then add details that look like lights or dials.

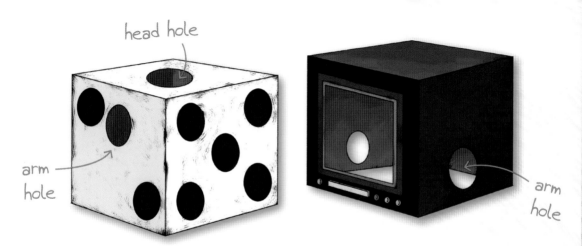

head hole

arm hole

arm hole

If you want your arms and upper body to be able to move freely, cut off the top and bottom of the box. Make shoulder straps by pressing two lengths of duct tape together. Then use more duct tape to attach these straps to the inside of the box in the front and back. Wear the box like overalls.

- *Present*: Paint the box to look like wrapping paper and a ribbon. Add tissue paper along the top edge of the box. You can be the surprise inside!
- *Jack-in-the-box*: Dress like a clown. Decorate the box in a circus theme. Draw a handle on the side.
- *Car*: Use a rectangular box. Paint a windshield, lights, doors, and other car details. Add round cardboard or felt circles to look like wheels.

Some of your costume ideas may not be shaped like a box. For these projects, cut two large pieces of cardboard from a box. Make sure they are the same size and shape. Connect them together with short duct tape straps. Wear the costume over your shoulders so that the cardboard hangs in the front and back. Here are some decorating ideas:

- *Pizza*: Cut the cardboard into triangle shapes. Paint and decorate it with pizza toppings!

- *Cell phone*: Paint the cardboard white and black, and then draw app icons on the cardboard "screen."

- *Book*: Draw or paint the cover of your favorite book on the cardboard. Add a large yarn tassel to look like a bookmark.

Sweatshirts and Sweatpants

Sweatshirts and sweatpants are a great base for many costumes. They come in lots of colors, and they are very comfortable. You can sew on details or attach them with a glue gun. You can also draw on your sweats using fabric paint.

- *Skeleton*: Start with a black sweatshirt and pants. Draw bones with white fabric paint. Some stores even carry glow-in-the-dark fabric paint.
- *Tiger or zebra*: Start with an orange or white set of sweats. Draw, paint, sew, or glue on black stripes.
- *Spider*: Use a black hooded sweatshirt. Cut two sets of two slots each in the back. Slide two black pool noodles into the slots to make the spider's legs. Sew eight red buttons near the front of the hood to make its eyes.

Plastic Headband and Chenille Sticks

A plain plastic headband is a good base for many head decorations.

- *Robot wires and bug antennae*: Twist two chenille sticks onto the headband. Wrap each chenille stick around a pencil. Remove the pencil and you will have a **coil** shape.

- *Tiara*: Attach four chenille sticks evenly spaced across the headband. Add beads, and then attach the ends to make a looped crown shape.

- *Animal ears*: Draw an ear shape on a piece of paper. Cut it out. Trace it onto felt twice, with the bottom of the ears touching. Cut out this shape. Fold it over the headband, and glue the two sides together. Repeat for other ear.

- *Animal mane*: Make a headband with animal ears. Cut a few chenille sticks in half. Twist them onto the headband, and coil them with a pencil.

Face Painting Tips

With just a little makeup, you can change your face to match your costume. Makeup is often a better choice than a mask when it is time to go trick-or-treating. It is much easier to see where you are going when you don't have a mask covering your eyes!

Materials
- Washable, nontoxic face paint
- Makeup sponges
- Soft paintbrushes
- Bowl of water
- Soap and water for cleanup

Steps
1. If you want to cover a large area of your face with color, dip a makeup sponge into a bit of water. Then pick up some paint on the sponge and wipe it over your face. Be careful not to get paint in your eyes or mouth.
2. To add details, dip a paintbrush in water and then in the color you want to use. Draw outlines and finer details.
3. It may be hard to paint on yourself, so ask a friend for help. You can practice on each other!

- *Spooky faces*: Painting your face white is a good way to look ghostly. Then you can add different details. Draw gray or black rings around your eyes. Draw dark lines on a white mouth to look like a skeleton, or red lips and fangs to look like a vampire. Add some cracked lines or red scars on your cheeks and forehead.
- *Animal faces*: Do a little research by looking at animal pictures. Think of the animal's face as shapes. Does it have a round nose or triangle nose? Does it have a round shape around its snout? What shape is its eyes? Are its eyebrows rounded, wavy, or triangular?

- *Fairy and princess faces:*
  Think pretty. Flowers, feathers,
  butterflies, jewels, shells, swirls,
  and curls all make good details for
  these faces. Focus on the eyes and
  the area around them. Make your face
  symmetrical. Paint the same thing on both
  sides of your face.
- *Other details:* You can add all sorts of details to your face
  to fit your costume. Freckles, beards, big lips, and rosy
  cheeks are easy to add using makeup. Instead of wearing
  a superhero mask or a pirate's eye patch, you can simply
  draw them on your face.

Hairy Spider

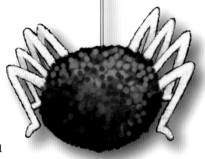

Pom-poms can easily be made into soft Halloween spiders. Make a bunch of these spiders to hang over a table or open doorway. You can also hang them outside in a tree to greet your Halloween guests.

Materials

- Thin cardboard (from a cereal box, for example)
- Ruler
- 1 skein of black yarn
- Scissors
- 4 gray chenille sticks
- Invisible thread

Steps

1. Cut a piece of cardboard that is about 5 inches (13 centimeters) long and 4 inches (10 cm) wide. Cut slots about 2 inches (5 cm) long into each of the cardboard's two short sides (make sure not to cut the cardboard into two separate pieces).
2. Wrap the yarn around the middle of the cardboard. Try to keep the cardboard flat as you wrap. Wrap the

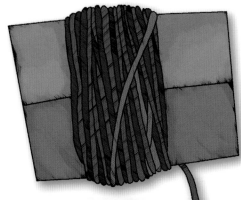

yarn about 75 to 100 times. Trim the end of the yarn when you are done.

3. Cut a piece of yarn that is about 12 inches (30 cm) long. Insert it into the slots on each side of the cardboard. Tie it as tight as you can around all the loops of yarn. Do not trim the tails of your piece of yarn.

4. Cut the ends of the yarn loops along one edge of the cardboard. Repeat on the other side.

5. Tear the cardboard in two to release your pom-pom.

6. Line up the chenille sticks. Twist them in the middle to hold them together. Tie them to the pom-pom with the tails of yarn. Then trim off the tails of yarn.

7. Flip over the pom-pom. Adjust the legs and bend the ends to look like feet.

8. To hang your spider, cut a long length of invisible thread. Tie the center of the thread around the middle of the spider. Then tie the ends together in a knot.

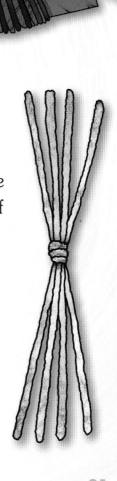

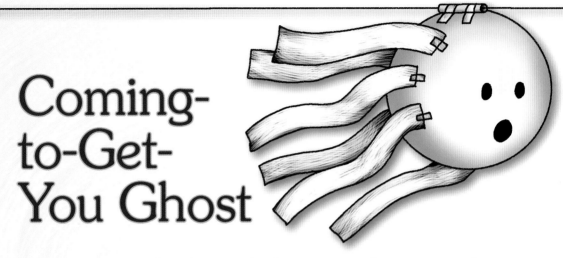

Coming-to-Get-You Ghost

Would you jump if a ghost rushed out at you from across the room? Surprise a friend with this simple trick. Boo!

Materials

- White balloon
- Binder clip
- Plastic straw
- Clear packing tape
- Black permanent marker
- White streamers
- 10 to 20 feet (3 to 6 meters) of string

Steps

1. Blow up a balloon. Don't tie the end. Instead, hold it closed with a binder clip.

2. Cut a 4-inch (10 cm) piece of the straw. Tape it to the side of the balloon.

3. Draw a spooky face on the top of the balloon.

4. Cut 12-inch (30 cm) lengths of streamers. Tape them around the face.

5. Tie or tape the string to one side of the room. Cut the string in a long enough piece to reach the other side of the room. Thread the end of the string through the straw on the balloon. The ghost's face should be facing the direction you want him to fly.

6. Pull the string across the room tightly, so it does not sag. Tape the string to the wall.

7. Release the clip, and your ghost will zip across the room! You can blow up the balloon again to reuse the ghost. If it pops, you can make another one!

ALL ABOUT THRUST
This trick is also a science experiment. The air rushing out of the balloon creates thrust. Thrust is a force that pushes the balloon in the opposite direction of the rushing air.

Eerie Eyes

Decorate your windows with these eerie, glowing eyes. Trick-or-treaters will wonder if your house is haunted!

Materials

- Large black paper
- Craft knife and cutting mat or scissors
- Vellum paper
- Invisible tape

Steps

1. Cut a piece of black paper the same size as your window. You can tape a few pieces together if you need to. Draw pictures of spooky eyes onto the paper. Cut them out with a craft knife. Be sure to use a cutting mat so you don't scratch your table or desk. If you

prefer, you can also use scissors to cut out the shape. If you use scissors, poke a hole in the center of the eye shape. Then cut from the center to the outer lines.

2. Flip the paper over. Tape the vellum onto the back of the black paper to cover all the eye holes.

3. Tape the paper to the window so that the vellum side is facing in. The black side should face out.

4. Place a lamp near the window. Turn out all the lights in the room except for the lamp. From outside your house, the eyes will seem to glow.

These eerie eyes will delight trick-or-treaters!

Hug Your Mummy!

Thousands of years ago, ancient Egyptians wrapped the bodies of their kings with linen cloth. These mummies have become a symbol of Halloween. But this smaller stuffed mummy is friendly. His bendable joints allow him to sit, stand, wave, or even hug.

Materials
- 6 chenille sticks
- Craft stick
- Cotton balls
- Masking tape
- White rags (such as fabric scraps or an old T-shirt)

Steps
1. Wrap the end of a chenille stick onto one end of the craft stick. Make a loop to create a head shape and then wrap the loose end of the chenille stick around the craft stick.
2. Wrap another chenille stick on the head end of the craft stick to make arms. Wrap two chenille sticks to the other end to make legs.

3. Tuck a handful of cotton balls into the head loop. Secure them loosely by wrapping them with masking tape.

4. Add a handful of cotton to make a belly. Wrap the cotton with some tape. Add cotton balls along each of the legs and arms, and wrap them loosely with tape.

5. To **reinforce** the arms and legs, wrap around them with two more chenille sticks.

6. Cut the rags into ½-inch (1 cm) strips. Starting at the arms, wrap the strips around and around until you have completely covered the chenille sticks, tape, and cotton balls. Tuck the ends in.

7. Continue wrapping strips around the head, body, and legs until your mummy is as plump as you would like him to be. Tuck in the ends of the rag strips.

8. Pose your mummy. (Or give him a hug!)

Rattling Chain

The clanking and shaking of chains is a scary sound on Halloween. Welcome trick-or-treaters to your home with a doorway decorated with chains. This **garland** gives your home a haunted look. You can also hang this chain from a chandelier or use it as part of a costume.

Material
- Heavy-duty aluminum foil

Steps
1. Tear off a piece of aluminum foil about 4 inches (10 cm) wide. Fold it up into a strip.
2. Scrunch and twist the foil so that it looks rough and uneven.
3. Loop the strip into a circle. Twist the end together to make the first chain link.
4. Repeat steps 1 and 2. Then thread the strip through the first chain link. Twist the ends together to make a second link.
5. Continue making links until your chain is the length you want.

The Creative Process

Halloween is one of the most creative holidays. But you can't just say "abracadabra" and transform yourself or your home for the holidays. You have to follow a creative process.

1. Imagine what you want to be or what you want to create. Get inspiration from the world around you.
2. Brainstorm ways to make your idea come to life. Ask yourself lots of questions. What supplies will you need? Will you have to buy materials or do you already have them? Will you need help from an adult?
3. Do some research. Look at pictures or objects to see how you can imitate them.
4. Draw out your ideas. You might make a sketch, a blueprint, or a list.
5. Experiment with your materials. You may find some ideas work while others don't. Making mistakes sometimes leads to even better ideas!
6. Make it happen. Take time to finish your project. Then show it off to your family and friends!

It's never too early to start thinking of ideas for next year's costume.

Glossary

coil (KOIL) a loop or series of loops

durable (DOOR-uh-buhl) tough and lasting for a long time

flexible (FLEK-suh-buhl) able to bend

garland (GAHR-luhnd) strand of flowers, leaves, or ornaments that people use for decoration

harvest (HAHR-vust) crops gathered at the end of the growing season

inspiration (in-spuh-RAY-shuhn) something that gives you a creative idea

reinforce (ree-in-FORS) to make something stronger or more secure

symmetrical (suh-MET-ri-kuhl) having matching parts or shapes on both sides of a dividing line

traditions (truh-DISH-uhnz) customs, ideas, or beliefs that are handed down from one generation to the next

translucent (trans-LOO-suhnt) not completely clear like glass, but able to let light through

For More Information

Books

Goldsworthy, Kaite. *Halloween*. New York: Weigl Publishers, 2012.

Marsh, Laura F. *Halloween*. Washington, D.C.: National Geographic, 2012.

Owen, Ruth. *Halloween Sweets and Treats*. New York: Windmill Books, 2013.

Rau, Dana Meachen. *Carving Pumpkins*. Ann Arbor, MI: Cherry Lake Publishing, 2012.

Web Sites

History Channel: Halloween

www.history.com/topics/halloween

Watch videos and read about the history of Halloween.

Pumpkin Carving 101

www.pumpkincarving101.com

Visit this site for lots of information about pumpkins and how to carve them.

Spoonful—Halloween Costume Ideas

http://spoonful.com/halloween/halloween-kids-costumes

This Disney site contains lots of fun ideas for Halloween costumes.

Index

About the Author

Dana Meachen Rau is the author of more than 300 books for children on many topics, including science, history, cooking, and crafts. She creates, experiments, researches, and writes from her home office in Burlington, Connecticut.